APPLE PENCIL 1 AND 2 BEGINNERS MANUAL
IN 30 MINUTES

A STEP- BY- STEP GUIDE TO PAIR AND USE APPLE'S FIRST AND SECOND GENERATION PENCILS

KONRAD
CHRISTOPHER

Copyright

Copyright©2020 Konrad Christopher

ISBN: 9798662984196

All rights reserved. No part of this book may be reproduced or used in any manner without the prior written permission of the copyright owner, except for the use of brief quotations in a book review.

While the advice and information in this book are believed to be true and accurate at the date of publication, neither the authors nor the editors nor the publisher can accept any legal responsibility for any errors or omissions that may be made. The publisher makes no warranty, express or implied, with respect to the material contained herein.

Printed on acid-free paper.

Printed in the United States of America
© 2020 by Konrad Christopher

Contents

Copyright i
INTRODUCTION 1
Second- Generation model 3
THE APPLE PENCIL 3
Apple Pencil vs Apple Pencil 2 4
How to connect an Apple Pencil 5
GETTING STARTED WITH APPLE PENCIL 6
PAIRING YOUR APPLE PENCIL (1ST GENERATION) WITH YOUR IPAD 7
CHARGING YOUR STYLUS 8
FIND THE BATTERY LIFE 8
PAIR YOUR APPLE PENCIL (2ND GENERATION) WITH YOUR IPAD 9
CHARGING YOUR APPLE PENCIL (1ST GENERATION) .. 12
CHARGING YOUR APPLE PENCIL (2ND GENERATION) 12
HOW TO REPLACE THE TIP 13
DRAW STRAIGHT LINES 14
HOW TO MAKE INSTANT NOTES ON SEVERAL NOTE APPS 15
IN-LINE MARK UP 22

HOW TO DRAG AND DROP	22
SCAN AND SIGN	23
APPLE PENCIL GESTURES	25
SELECT TEXT AND MENU ITEMS	27
HOW TO TRACE	28
THIRD-PARTY APPS ON iOS	30
HOW TO USE WORKS WITH ARKIT	35
CAPTURE A NOTE FROM LOCKSCREEN	42
BEST APPS FOR APPLE PENCIL	44
HOW TO STORE YOUR PENCIL	45
LEARN HOW TO DRAW WITH IPAD AND APPLE PENCIL	48
LEARN HOW TO DRAW FROM THE MASTERS	49
HOW TO MARKUP AN EMAIL WITH THE APPLE PENCIL	51
HOW TO USE APPLE PENCIL WITH OFFICE 365 INK FEATURE ON YOUR IPAD PRO	53
WHEN YOU SHOULD REPLACE YOUR APPLE PENCIL NIB	56
HOW DO I REPLACE MY APPLE PENCIL TIP?	57
CONCLUSION	58

About the Author 60

INTRODUCTION

Apple pencil can be described as a line of wireless stylus pen ancillary created and patterned by Apple Inc. to be utilized with supported iPad tablets.

The first generation Apple Pencil was revealed with the first- generation iPad Pro on the 9th of September, 2015. The pencil is backed up by the first and second-generation iPad Pro patterns, the sixth generation iPad put out in 2018, alongside the 2019 releases of iPad Air, iPad Mini, and iPad. It passes signal wirelessly through Bluetooth, and possesses a detachable cap that conceals a Lightning connector utilized for charging purposes.

A second edition was released in 2018, which is utilized on the third and fourth generation iPad Pro models. It utilizes an attractable connector on the side of the tablet for charging instead of a physical connection, and involves touch-sensitive regions that can be clicked to carry out actions within supported applications.

Apple began to sell refurbished Apple Pencil (2nd generation) ancillaries at $109 in April 2020.

The Apple Pencil possesses angle detection and pressure sensitivity, and was patterned for low latency to make room for smooth marking on the screen. However, the Pencil and the user's fingers can be utilized concurrently, while declining input from the user's palm. One angle of the device possesses a magnetically- fastened detachable cap. Just below the cap is the Lightning connector, which lets the Pencil's battery to be recharged through an iPad's Lightning port itself. The initial charge sustains for about 12 hours, but 15 seconds connected into the Lightning connector of the iPad offers abundant power for 30 minutes of use.

Apple has however advanced the Pencil as being tailored towards productivity and creative work; in the course of its release, the pen's capabilities were illustrated using the mobile version of Adobe Photoshop, and its credential annotation capabilities on various Microsoft Office apps.

The Apple Pencil utilizes a STMicroelectronics STM32L151UCY6 Ultra-low power 32-bit RISC ARM-centered Cortex-M3-MCU working at 32 MHz alongside 64kb of flash memory, a Bosch Sensortech BMA280 3-axis accelerometer and a Cambridge Silicon Radio VSR1012A05 Bluetooth Smart IC for its Bluetooth connection to the iPad. It is strengthened by a rescuable recyclable 3.82 V, 0.329 Wh lithium-ion battery.

Second- Generation model

Apple released an advanced model of the Pencil as well as the third-generation iPad Pro. It is the same in design and stipulations to the first model, but lacking the removable connector, and having a segment of the stylus to aid rolling. It entails click-sensitive regions on its side that may be located to function within apps.

Instead of a physical Lightning connector, the second generation Pencil is charged utilizing a magnetic wireless charging connector on the tablet. So, it is only backed up by the third- generation and fourth-generation (2020) iPad pro. These models had likewise swapped to USB-C connectors due to Lightning, enabling their compatibility with the first generation Pencil. Succeeding non-Pro iPad patterns or models, including the third generation iPad Air, 2019 10.2-inch iPad (which do not entail the attractable connector, and still utilizing Lightning over USB-C, and the fifth-generation iPad Mini have only backed up the first generation Pencil pattern.

THE APPLE PENCIL

An Apple Pencil remains one of the best pieces of kit you can purchase for your new iPad, in order to make the most of the slate by permitting you to doodle, sketch, handwrite, annotate and more.

The original Apple Pencil and the Apple Pencil 2 launched in 2015 and 2018 respectively, allow you to replace your wobble finger with an accurate and slender stylus, which is essential for many workers and creatives alike.

Price and Availability

You can access an Apple Pencil from Apple's website, and it is often the same price as purchasing the same from a third-party retailer, but you can get the Apple Pencil 2 there freely.

You will purchase the original Apple Pencil at $99, while the Apple Pencil is a bit higher at $129. Also, the styluses function well with several tablets, so choosing the right Apple Pencil is not just about choosing the one in your price range.

Apple Pencil vs Apple Pencil 2

The decision to choose either of the two is easy to take. Perhaps you have a 2018 model iPad Pro 11 or iPad Pro 12.9, you should consider the Apple Pencil 2, but the original stylus functions with the older iPad Pro versions alongside newer iPads in other ranges.

There are some main differences between the older and newer Apple Pencils. The Apple Pencil 2 sticks magnetically to the side of your iPad, and charges wirelessly when it is properly set; therefore, it is very easy to use. In addition, the original Apple Pencil can be charged when plugged in to the table, therefore it is far fiddler to power up.

The Apple Pencil on the other hand also has a double-click function, so in some particular apps, you can speedily press the lower portion of the stylus two times to switch back to the former tool you were utilizing. This double-click feature can be positioned to display the color palette or activate the eraser.

How to connect an Apple Pencil

When compared to some other peripherals like wearables or headphones, an Apple Pencil is amazingly easy to link to your slate, as your iPad will automatically do most of the work.

Firstly, ensure Bluetooth is turned on, on your iPad, otherwise the stylus won't function. To achieve this, access the main 'Settings' menu, or pull down the 'Control Center', and turn on 'Bluetooth' if it is not on already.

For the original Apple Pencil, withdraw the cap at the end to show the Lightning Connector and plug this into the Lightning Port on your iPad. Simply link the stylus to the attractable strip on your iPad Pro, while using the Apple Pencil2. Automatically, the Apple Pencil 2 will pair but for the original, you have to click a prompt first.

Worthy of note is the fact that with the original Apple Pencil, if you turn off the iPad, switch to the airplane mode, or link the Apple Pencil to a different iPad, you will have to go through the pairing process all over again.

GETTING STARTED WITH APPLE PENCIL

Apple's Notes app remains the perfect way to begin utilizing the Apple Pencil. Make a new note, and then click the 'Markup' icon at the bottom right of the screen.

Notes show a collection of tools at the bottom of the screen. You can now start drawing or writing text. The iPad Pro provides perfect Palm Rejection so it does not think you are writing or drawing with your whole hand.

You have an option of colors with black and the basic colors instantly ready, click the 'Color Wheel' to select a different color.

You can also utilize the 'Eraser Tool' either by clicking it in the tools palette or by double-clicking the device if you have set that option- to remove anything you have drawn.

However, you can utilize the 'Selection Tool' to choose an element, then click and drag it to a new place. The selection tool does not offer you a fine selection; it chooses entire objects that you have drawn. Also, note that the Redo and Undo icons at the bottom left of the screen lets you step backward and forward in your actions.

PAIRING YOUR APPLE PENCIL (1ST GENERATION) WITH YOUR IPAD

Before you commence, ensure you have the Apple Pencil model that functions well with your iPad. Also, you might need to get your Apple Pencil charged before using it.

Withdraw the cap and plug your Apple Pencil into the Lightning connector right on your iPad.

When you can see the Pair Button, click it.

After you have gotten the Apple Pencil paired, it will remain paired until you start your iPad again, switch on Airplane mode, or pair with another iPad. Pair your Apple Pencil all over again whenever you are ready to use it.

CHARGING YOUR STYLUS

To charge your stylus, insert the micro USB into the base of your Pencil and plug it into an outlet. The red light turns on for a second or two, after which it goes off. Based on the battery size, the pen should be completely charged after 1.1 hours.

FIND THE BATTERY LIFE

Although the second generation Apple Pencil magnetically joins and charges on the side of your iPad Pro or iPad, worthy of note is how to check the battery status of your Apple Pencil, most especially, when the Apple Pencil has been in use for a long time.

To check Apple Pencil battery life:

- Examine the batteries widget by swiping from left to right, right from your Home screen.

- Perhaps you cannot find a battery widget, move down, click Edit, and press the + symbol situated next to the Batteries icon.
- You may have to charge your Apple Pencil if you don't see the battery widget or perhaps the battery widget is not signaling the battery life.

The percentage of the battery will display in a bubble at the top of your screen when you join it to the side of the Apple Pencil.

PAIR YOUR APPLE PENCIL (2ND GENERATION) WITH YOUR IPAD

Rightly connecting your Apple Pencil to the attractable connector on the side of your iPad Pro.

On an Apple Pencil (2nd generation), you can double click the lower segment of Apple Pencil to speedily swap back to the tool you utilized last. To adjust your settings for double-click, go to Settings > Apple Pencil, then select among:

- Swap between current tool and eraser
- Swap between current tool and last utilized
- Display color palette
- Off.

However, if your Apple Pencil wont successfully pair with your iPad:

- Ensure you center your Apple Pencil on the attractable connector on the right edge of your iPad
- Reboot your iPad, then attempt pairing again
- Go to Settings > Bluetooth and ensure that Bluetooth is switched on.
- Check under 'My Devices' for your Apple Pencil, right on the same screen. Click the encircled 'I' if you see it. Then click 'Forget this Device'.
- Link your Apple Pencil to your iPad and click the pair button when it displays after some seconds.
- If you can't see the pair button, be patient for about one minute while your Apple Pencil charges. Then attempt linking your Apple Pencil again and wait until you can see the pair button.

If you don't see the pair button after the outlined procedures, you might need to contact Apple Support.

To adjust the double-click function for the second-generation Apple Pencil:

- Access 'Settings' on your iPad Pro
- Click 'Apple Pencil'
- Click 'Switch Between Current Tool and Eraser', 'Switch between Current Tool and Lost Used', 'Show Color Palette' or 'Off'.

- Double-click to switch modes on the second-generation Apple Pencil

The most recent generation of the Apple Pencil comes with a flat surface that you can double-click in order to change between tools. Perhaps you are drawing or writing with the Apple Pencil and make a mistake, double-click the surface to change to the eraser tool in your current app and delete the error, or utilize the double-click to change between your present and former tools.

USING THE APPLE PENCIL

You can utilize your Apple Pencil to markup, write and draw with preloaded apps and apps from the App Store. Using some apps like Notes, you can draw and chalk out utilizing an Apple Pencil.

With iPadOS, shift the redesigned tool palette around the screen or denigrate it so you have more room to draw and sketch. Utilize the ruler tool to make straight lines, and then move them around with your fingers.

To draw or chalk out in the Notes app:

- Access Notes
- Click the enclosed pencil icon to begin a new note

- To draw, click the encircled pencil icon, if you can't find it, advance your notes. To sketch, click the colored encircled pencil icon.

Commence your drawing or sketch. You can select from various drawing tools and colors, and swap to the eraser perhaps you make a mistake. Double click the Eraser to see erasing alternatives on your iPad. When you draw or sketch, you can slant your Apple Pencil to shade a line and enforce more firmly to get the line darkened.

CHARGING YOUR APPLE PENCIL (1ST GENERATION)

Connect your Apple Pencil into the Lightning connector on your iPad to charge. You can also choose to charge with a USB Power Adapter by utilizing the Apple Pencil Charging Adapter that was in-built in your Apple Pencil.

The Apple Pencil will charge faster when plugged into either of the discussed power sources.

CHARGING YOUR APPLE PENCIL (2ND GENERATION)

The way the Apple Pencil, 2nd generation is charged is different from the way the 1st generation is charged.

Connect your Apple Pencil to the attractable connector at the center of the upper part of the iPad- the side with the volume buttons. Ensure that the Bluetooth is turned on if you don't see the charge status display for some time near the top of the screen.

To check your charge status:

- When you connect an Apple Pencil (2nd generation) to your iPad, the charge status will appear on the screen for a moment.
- To view how much charge your Apple Pencil has left while you are utilizing it, access the 'Today View' on your iPad. Just swipe from left to right on the Lock screen or Home screen.

HOW TO REPLACE THE TIP

Similar to a standard pencil, the Apple Pencil tip will have to be replaced from time to time, particularly when you use your Apple Pencil frequently.

To replace your Apple Pencil tip:

- Get hold of your Apple Pencil, and wriggle the Apple Pencil tip counter-clockwise
- After a few wriggle, the tip should totally come off, revealing the golden pins underneath
- Get hold of your Apple Pencil tip and wriggle it clockwise into your present Apple Pencil. Ensure the tip is firmly secured but don't over- tighten.

- Test run your Apple Pencil with your iPad.

PRESSURE-SENSING CAPABILITIES

A line can be thinner or thicker. The outcome of your drawing depends largely on how much pressure you place on the iPad while drawing or writing. Apple does not offer a particular pressure sensing capability for the Apple Pencil.

PALM REJECTION

This is a feature of the Apple Pencil that denotes that when the Apple Pencil is linked to the iPad, it does not recognize your hand or finger but your Apple Pencil tip, giving you room to write or sketch with comfort.

Your arm, hand and fingers can rest on the screen when you draw with Apple Pencil, thanks to this feature. While former third-party styluses have had fluctuations on Palm Rejection in some apps, they never worked excellently; the Apple Pencil, in opposition, is about as excellent as Palm Rejection as you can be with a digital Touchscreen.

DRAW STRAIGHT LINES

The simplest way to get a straight line drawn with Apple Pencil is to use the ruler in the Notes App. Access the Ruler, position it where you need it to be, and utilize the Pencil to draw just along the straight edge.

INSTANT MARKUP

Capture a screenshot and you can include all types of annotation right in the screenshot preview screen.

You can also simply markup other items, such as attachments in images or mail, photos, just click them with your Pencil first.

HOW TO MAKE INSTANT NOTES ON SEVERAL NOTE APPS

You wonder about that feature that allows you to open and write a Note by clicking the iPad's lock screen? You get it activated in Settings>Notes>Access Notes from Lock Screen, and position it to always make a new note, resume Last Notes accessed in the app, or resume last Note accessed from the Lock Screen.

To instantly create a note, wake your iPad, and then click the 'Lock screen' with your Apple Pencil. Click a 'Tool' and begin sketching or writing. You can reset the Toolbar by dragging it to any edge as you work.

NOTES APP

As regards Apple's launch of the iPad mini 5 and the iPad Air 3, all new model iPad devices backup Apple Pencil. That is, the iPad Air, 9.7-inch iPad, iPad mini and iPad Pro. Either you need to take handwritten notes, record audio, annotate documents, create sports playbooks, or more, the App Store possesses a number of amazing apps for note-taking. Some of the apps are discussed below:

- **Notes App**

Perfectly fitting for the use of Apple Pencil is the iPad's default Notes app. It possesses inline scanning and annotation, text recognition search, and sketching or handwriting support. You can designate the double-click tool to either erase or the last tool utilized with your Apple Pencil 2. It has more confined features than the best third-party notes app- you can't sync your notes anywhere else aside from iCloud, and there is no way to connect several notes together. Perhaps you are sketching an idea or jotting down a quick note, the Notes app is that excellent quick-hit app. Similar to having a napkin with you all the time.

- **Notability App**

This is the perfect app for general note-taking, and it doubles as a fan favorite of various note-taking aficionados. It has a perfect interface occupied with tools for drawing, handwriting, making shapes, annotating PDFs, moving objects around, highlighting, incorporating photos and web clips, adding audio, and a lot more. Perhaps you want a more real experience with your note-taking, you can select a number of different paper styles, involving grids, which is very essential for vector line drawing. Also, you can share your notebooks to just about all major services and print them, as well as importing notebooks from Google Drive, Dropbox, or a WebDAV service. This app also provides iCloud sync backup and a companion Mac app.

Because it is rich in features, it can be a little complex to new users. Interestingly, this app offers a really helpful tutorial to guide you through its features when you first access it.

This app however functions seamlessly with the Apple Pencil, either you are sketching, writing, or drawing shapes. It is a perfect, well-designed app if you desire more power than what the default Notes app offers.

GoodNotes.

This is an advanced app for note-taking. It is perfect for the power-utilizing note-takers. It is packed to the full with a rich list of pro features.

For new users, this app provides a truly massive selection of paper kinds for its digital notebooks, including graph, lined, design and music notation; there are also improved options that allow you to upload custom templates. However, most templates are available in particular paper sizes, perhaps you are working for print. GoodNotes also provides a ton of several cover types and options, all of which you can write upon and further design.

Similar to other apps in its category, GoodNotes backs up drawing and writing with the Apple Pencil, as well as a number of third-party stylus options, utilizing two different digital writing tools: a digital fountain or ball pen in a custom or preset color spectrum.

This app also possesses pre-loaded handwriting Search Recognition and Text Conversion, which is done through MyScript's engine which also powers MyScript Nebo.

- **OneNote**

Microsoft's note application is more of a note storing reservoir than a full-featured note-taking application. Furthermore, it has a lot of features for iPad users with an Office 365 subscription, which allows you to import and edit documents freely. You don't necessarily need a Skype or Microsoft account to enjoy these features.

With this app, you can share links to your notebooks to others, annotate documents with your Apple Pencil and email a PDF of your notebook to the public. In one note, you can sketch an idea, add audio and photos, create calendars, type notes and a lot more. This app is similar to Evernote but this is developed to function seamlessly with Office 365.

- **PDF Expert**

This app is the king of PDF markup and annotation. Although you can speedily edit, highlight and markup PDFs on your iPad utilizing the preloaded Markup extension, if you need to frequently annotate PDF files, PDF Expert might be the perfect option for you. It contains a list of advanced markup tools to make things much easier for you. You can access PDFs from iCloud or any other online service with the PDF Expert app, sign documents, fill out forms; you can also work with items with a digital pen, underline, shape tool, highlighter option or strike-thru, alongside creating stamps for often-used wording. All the changes made to your document are not only fully editable in PDF Expert, but also in applications like Preview and Adobe Acrobat- so you can move from Mac to your Personal Computer and back again with your iPad.

PDF Expert also allows you to edit the structure of PDFs themselves. You can choose to delete sections, rearrange pages, extract parts of the PDF, and even include new blank pages to your documents. Immediately you are through with a PDF document, you can also zip it using PDF Expert preloaded compressor and password-protect crucial documents.

Perhaps you desire to tinker with your PDFs, PDF Expert provides a Pro upgrade in-app that lets you to physically edit the images, text, and links inside a PDF, as well as adapt information.

- **MyScript Nebo**

This is the perfect app for you if you need handwriting recognition. Perhaps you desire converting your scribbles to text, you will need an app that backs up handwriting conversion. Apps like GoodNotes and Notes scan your text for search purposes, but don't provide outright handwriting recognition. Taking a step further, apps like MyScript Nebo provide full handwriting-to-text conversion.

MyScript is a big name in handwriting recognition, but it remains the company's first try at an app developed and designed for Apple Pencil and iPad Pro. The app is easy to utilize and provides a silky-smooth digital pen tool in different colors. Also, users can include diagrams, photographic and video content and equations, aside from handwriting or digital text.

MyScript Nebo notebooks can be converted into a paragraph or a full notebook at a time. Those conversions are non-destructive, but you can preserve the handwriting version perhaps the conversion is not perfect. Also, you can export notebooks as HTML, text, word documents or PDF. Sync is available via MyScript's copyrighted service, including Google Drive, iCloud, Dropbox.

- **LiquidText**

This app is free with in-app purchases. This app remains a great concept for annotating and organizing PDFs but it is too narrow to be taken as an equal to PDF Expert.

- **Notes Plus**

This is a great entry in the handwriting recognition class with back up for Apple Pencil. Nevertheless, the app is a bit clumsier in the looks phase with iffy Palm Rejection.

- **EverNote**

This app is costless with in-app subscription. Similar to Microsoft's OneNote, Evernote remains a fabulous import repository for organizing a ton of notes, data, sketches and documents. To explore its rich sync capabilities, PDF annotation and a lot more, you will need to purchase the subscription plan. This app is great if you need all the advantages and features a subscription offer, but not quite worth jumping in for the costless edition.

- **Noteshelf**

This app brings together many amazing features from GoodNotes and Notability, including custom page templates and audio recordings, but the writing tool is not as impressive.

- **Whink**

This is an amazing entry-level handwriting application, and it is quite cool, providing audio and photo incorporation, nice pen tool, and basic document annotation. However, the stock Notes application is a better general recommendation for most users.

IN-LINE MARK UP

Comment on an image, webpage or document on your iPad. Utilize your Apple Pencil to swipe up from the bottom corner, to capture the screen. Select a tool from the Markup toolbar, then begin sketching or writing.

HOW TO DRAG AND DROP

You can drag and drop several items utilizing the Apple Pencil. All you have to do is click something with the Pencil to select it and you can click add-on items with your finger, adding all these to a stack you can easily move around with your stylus.

SCAN AND SIGN

Swipe up from the bottom corner of the screen to create a signature with Apple Pencil. Click + in the Markup toolbar, select 'Signature', sign your name, then click 'Done'.

The subsequent time you need a signature, click + in the toolbar of a backed up app, then click Signature to include your signature and position it in the document. Perhaps you are utilizing an IPad Pro, you can utilize the Apple Pencil to get a more accurate edition of your signature than what you will most likely obtain by signing with your finger.

Amidst the abundance of new features presented with the launch of iOS 11 was the improvement on the preloaded Notes app, which now permits you to speedily and easily capture documents with your iPad and iPhone camera. You can then decide to comment on or sign the documents with the Note app's preloaded markup tools.

You don't have to pass through the strenuous process of printing a document on paper, signing it and scanning it again, with this novel feature.

Access the Notes app and start a new note. Then click +button, and select Scan document. That accesses your device's camera. Just before pointing the camera at your documents, you can change some settings - to either turn on the flashlight or not, capture the document in grayscale, color, black and white or as a full photo. Whichever option you choose, you will be able to adjust it after capturing the image. Also, you can select between the manual and auto capture.

With the auto setting, the scanner will take a photo when it finds the whole document in the frame. You will have to click the shutter button to switch to manual.

To obtain the best results from your scans, ensure the document is placed on a flat surface, and that there is sufficient contrast between the surface and the document. Then hold your device as near as possible to the document while ensuring the document is onscreen.

In auto mode, a yellow highlight shows around the document as it is being found, and in just a few seconds, you will hear a shutter sound as it captures a photo. Perhaps you have various pages to scan, position the next page in view and hold your device over it again. Keep performing this process all over until all the pages are captured.

Immediately you are through, click the save button. Your scanned pages now display in the note you created. Click the scanned pages to access them in editing mode.

APPLE PENCIL GESTURES

There might be more Apple Pencil gestures in store for future generations of Apple's iPad stylus. The first of these was seen in the second-generation device, in the form of a double click to speedily access the tools.

Currently, you can personalize this gesture to do one of four things:

- Fire up the settings app
- Move down to Apple Pencil. Click on it
- You will have four options to select from.
- A novel Apple patent application spotted by Pocket Lint takes this quite some steps further.

First, it defines additional gestures, such as a triple-click, a rolling gesture and a swiping motion.

The touch sensor can be utilized to discover a click, double-click, triple-click or another click gesture by the user. The stylus as a user's click gesture can decode the frequency of input within a period. Discovered click gestures can be related with preprogrammed functions to be carried out by the stylus or/ and external device upon the discovery of the click gestures. For instance, one or more clicks can be decoded as a user input to adjust a feature of a marking created by use of the stylus with the external device. By further example, one or more clicks can be decoded as a user input to carry out functions on the external device, such as a paste function, a copy function, an undo function, or/and a redo function. By further instance, one or more clicks can be decoded as a user input to adjust a tool setting for creating markings on the external device. The user can utilize the touch sensor to discover a sliding gesture. The touch sensor can also be utilized to discover a rolling gesture by the user. It can however include movement of a finger about a circumference of the housing or/and rolling movement of the housing.

Secondly, it suggests that a capacitive sensor, same to that utilized on an iPhone screen or most Touch ID buttons, would only respond to intentional gestures.

A stylus containing a housing defining a grip area of the stylus; and a capacitive touch sensor containing several sensing elements dispatched circumferentially and longitudinally along an inner surface of the housing right at the grip area, wherein the capacitive touch sensor is set up to discover movement of a finger with regard to the grip area while the grip area is held by other fingers.

Thirdly, the patent encompasses all the bases in terms of other input devices that could be integrated, including a camera.

The external device can include one or more of a memory, a processor, one or more sensors, a power supply, one or more data connectors, one or more communication interfaces, one or more input/output devices, one or more power connectors, such as a microphone, a speaker, a rotary input device, an on/off button, a biometric sensor, a mute button, a camera, a force or/and touch sensitive trackpad, and the list continues.

This last one is almost definitely just Apple's patent lawyers encompassing all the bases rather than anything we are most likely to see in reality. On the other hand, more Apple Pencil gestures seem eminently commendable.

SELECT TEXT AND MENU ITEMS

The Apple Pencil is the easiest way to select text when working on an iPad. Click and hold to select a word and you should see highlights show on that word, with double dots at either side. To choose more words on either side of the chosen, just utilize your Pencil to choose a dot and broaden the chosen area. It is far more accurate than using a finger for the same purpose.

HOW TO TRACE

Do you know you can actually write on your iPad via paper utilizing your Apple Pencil? Yes, standard printer paper should be suitable. This is particularly essential if you want to trace something into a drawing app.

It is as easy as it sounds to speedily trace an outline of an image onto iPad Pro using your Apple Pencil.

First, you need to select an app, before you start considering apps like Procreate, Paper by Fifty-Three, Procreate, or Adobe Sketch. However, Apple's own Notes app can be sufficient for this.

Two physical things need to be done before utilizing the software for this. Firstly, turn up the brightness on your iPad Pro's screen. Though you will be running the Apple Pencil over paper atop that screen, you need to have it bright in order to see what you have done and whatever is left to trace.

Secondly, you will find a way to fasten down the paper to the iPad. That requires more tricks than it sounds because you won't want to damage the iPad and perhaps you are working with an original document, you won't want to have that damaged either. However, you must fasten it because the iPad Pro glass is too smooth for this. Your paper will move just as you run the Pencil over it. You could also attempt weighting down either side of the paper if it's bigger than your screen, or you could probably attempt Post-It-notes.

Follow these steps so that the paper stays steady but don't do it so that you have to undo everything at every time you need to adjust a control on the iPad.

Controls.

You will keep the paper steady, but also not too locked down that you can't access the app controls. Either you will forget to change the app from handwriting or typing to sketching, or something you do will make the iPad adjust the tool for you.

The most infuriating thing we discovered was when a finger press accidentally changes the tool we were utilizing or would restrain a line we were trying to draw, making it absolutely straight when we were trying to follow a contour.

Perhaps you fail

Tracing with iPad Pro and Apple Pencil is not to be done in haste. Obviously, it is tremendously slower than just scanning a document. Perhaps you have constraint access to the image or document; it is advisable you take a photograph of it with your iPad's camera just in case.

Then, if you really cannot trace neatly with the Pencil, take the photograph to a Mac and into a tool like Adobe Illustrator. This possesses a feature called Live Trace, which changes any image into line art.

After turning the entire image into line art, you will need to go through with a very fine eraser to pick out the details you don't want.

However, as much as it is difficult to stop in the middle of a trace, it is advisable you stop often. Lift the paper and share what you have done so far. You will erase something you don't want and you will make mistakes in the tracing. If you notice them right away, you can lift the page and click on the app's undo button.

THIRD-PARTY APPS ON iOS

The request for iPhone News Alert is always huge despite the fact that there are several mobile phones available in the market. With the launch of the iPhone, more people are on the lookout for these types of phones that makes life easy and better for them. They are mostly used in enterprises and for entertainment purposes. Apple News Alert is coming out with more innovative features to sustain it amidst competitions in the tech via the introduction of new generation mobile phones.

Mobile applications that fit the iPhone will have perfect features that the customer will benefit from. The most recent developments and innovation in internet technology have attracted people to bank more on hand-held applications than what was obtainable. Nowadays, we practically do any work utilizing internet tools. Handheld gadgets have become inevitable since the cataclysmic evolution of internet-based technology. Obviously, mobile phones with no applications are almost nothing. We are long past the times when the development of application was deemed to be intense, similar to any other development task. Today, it is easy to create an enterprising mobile application that is compacted with a user-friendly interface and essential tools in its stock.

However, Official App Stores have rigid policies for downloading mobile apps. On the other hand, online users are always looking out for superior solutions to meet their day-to-day needs. The answer therefore comes in the form of Third-Party App Stores. These stores have developed with time, making it possible and easy for users to discover, download and install what meets their desire.

Regulations and policies bind the devices. Premium packages end up as paid editions. Developers have grabbed the opportunity to create free or very cheap yet quality premium applications, as options for the official releases. The applications almost achieved what the real version was meant for, and in some cases, even better. Although they are not always legitimate in the eyes of the stellar corporations, overtime, they have turned to be legitimate and trustworthy. Furthermore, online users have always enjoyed simple applications, with reduced policy fuss and costless to use, packaged with excellent user experience. However, the need for easily identifiable and downloadable apps is the most important factor for dynamic third-party application development.

The third-party apps also assist us to utilize the iOS platform for testing and developing apps that seamlessly function on thousands of iOS devices. In that way, it increases your workforce, which in turn results in an increase in productivity and collaboration to reach the partners and consumers.

Android News Alert users have enjoyed the most from Third-Party App Stores, traditionally. Apple devices are known to be strict in permitting third-party applications to work. The iOS operating system has a standout blocker system, which reduces the capability to find and install Third-Party Stores. Recent developments however, have made iOS users to find Third-Party App Stores and download their needed applications by masking the device's blocker system. This development might be responsible for the paradigm shift from Android to iOS systems for several online users. The following are the kingpins of the online world, from the several Third-Party App Stores available for iOS.

AppValley

TweakBox

iOSEmus

TutuApp

Aptoide

Emus4U

Into Cydia/iNoJB

GetJar

There is a good chance for each user to access, download and install the above-mentioned apps and enjoy the advantages to a reasonable extent, with an available IOS mobile app. You can be confident that no issue will prop up as regards the security of your phone at the time of using these mobile apps. AppValley remains one of the best third-party apps for IOS. Your process can be made very easy with the aid of the above-mentioned app.

There are a lot of benefits, functionalities and options available in these third-party mobile application stores, and it is easy for users to select the right store fitting for their needs. Users desiring different models, rare applications, and advanced premium features freely can utilize the third-party app stores to access their desired choice of application. Essentially, as earlier stated, each and everything up for grabs is at no cost. There are also news feeds to give you updates on new offerings and latest releases. Third-party apps can be easily discovered and downloaded via regular browser searches. Routine application and simple profile creation are just about enough to get your desired gadget application downloaded. Also, a committed customer support team is always available to resolve queries and concerns.

Therefore, if you can't afford the original application, third-party app stores are your one-stop solution to have the premium content downloaded for free.

HOW TO USE WORKS WITH ARKIT

At the Apple's Worldwide Developer Conference (WWDC) in San Jose, California, Apple unveiled 'ARKit", a new costless set of software tools that we can utilize to create amazing new apps and experiences on the iPad and iPhone. The 'AR' in 'ARKit' means 'Augmented Reality', a technology that positions interactional virtual objects and effects into your perspective of the real world, creating a blend between the virtual world and the physical reality.

Today, this is often achieved by apps that utilize a smartphone's camera to reveal to you a glimpse of the real world in front of you, then layering virtual objects on top of it. For instance, some of the most commonly utilized AR features currently are the face filters or 'lenses' in Snapchat- the upshot or effects that place animal ears on your head or display your face in strange ways. Another app in this category is Pokeman Go, the gaming app that made the pocket monsters appear as if they were moving around the street or your desk. What is common to these apps is that the virtual objects inside of them seem inhabiting or altering real world scenes- 'augmenting' our reality.

What makes Apple's ARKit version of augmented reality so amazing is that it is not an app- it is rather a free way for anybody to build or create novel AR apps that will be able to work on many Apple's iOS devices. Discussed below are the ways to get started.

- Check to ensure you have a compatible iOS device.
- ARKit works on only Apple iOS devices possessing an A9 processor or newer, that restricts it to the following devices:

iPhone 6s and 6s plus

iPhone SE

iPhone 7 and 7 plus

iPad Pro (9.7, 10.5 or 12.9)

iPad (2017)

Presumptively, the new iPhone 8 lineup will also backup ARKit. You will also want to ensure the camera on your iOS device is functioning because ARKit depends upon it. And you also need a cable for linking your device to your Mac computer.

- **Download iOS 11 on your iPhone or iPad**

As soon as you have one of these agreeable iOS devices handy, you will have to download iOS 11 on it. That is the newest version of Apple's mobile operating system, and it is accessible only as a beta currently, which means it invariably possesses bugs and could mess some things up on your device.

- **Check to ensure you have a compatible Mac computer**

You will sure need a computer for coding your ARKit app, particularly, a Mac with the free operating system Mac OS Sierra 10.12.4 (or newer edition) installed. That implies the following machines are suitable:

MacBook (Late 2009 or newer)

MacBook Air (Late 2010 or newer)

MacBook Pro (Mid 201 or newer)

iMac (Late 2009 or newer)

Mac mini (Mid 2010 or newer)

Mac Pro (Mid 2010 or newer)

- **Register for an Apple Developer account**

You can use a costless or paid developer account to start using ARKit. Perhaps you already have a regular consumer account that you often utilize to purchase apps and such on your iPad/iPhone/Mac, you can advance this to a free or paid developer account. Utilizing a web browser on your Mac computer, move to Apple's developer account sign-in page and select the right option for you.

Download Xcode 9 freely (which has ARKit) for your Mac from Apple's developer website.

Right on your Mac, sign in into your Apple developer account, then tap 'download' at the top right corner to access Xcode 9, Apple's program for programming.

- **Launch Xcode 9 and link your iOS device to your computer using a cable**

Right on your Mac, access your Xcode 9 download by tapping it twice, then drag the Xcode app into your Applications folder and tap it twice to launch it. Plug in the iOS device you have with iOS 11 installed.

- **Make a new AR app project templates in Xcode**

In Xcode on your Mac, tap 'File', 'New' and choose 'Project'. This would pop up a number of options. Tap 'Augmented Reality App'.

- **Fill out your new AR app's information in Xcode**

Apple requires you to fill out the following information for your novel AR app. You can of course give it any name you desire and ensure you also choose a 'Team', even if you are an individual. Ensure you check every other thing.

In the 'Language' option, you can select between Swift- Apple's new programming language, and Objective-C- its older one. Both will permit you to build an AR app. Swift might be the better option as it is what Apple intends using for all its tools going forward, especially if you are new to programming.

On a final note, you can select your 'Content Technology', choosing between Scenekit, Metal and SpriteKit. These are distinguishable rendering engines for getting graphics displayed. All three will allow you to build AR apps, but provide differing trade-offs. You can also choose anywhere you want, as you will need to put up your project in a folder on your personal computer.

- **Choose your connected or linked iOS device to get your new AR app**

In Xcode on your Mac, choose 'Window' from the top menu bar; tap 'Devices and Simulators' and double tap your iOS device. Ensure you check the box that says, "Show as Run Destination".

You might get a pop up on your iOS device saying "Untrusted Developer" and offering some guidelines to go to your iOS device's Settings page to permit this app. Perhaps this happens, go ahead and get the 'Settings' app on your iOS device, click it, scroll down to 'General' and click it, then move forward to 'Profiles and Device Management', and you should be able to get your Apple developer email address. Click this and it should permit you to get your ARapp installed.

- **Run your first demo AR app**

Apple lets in a very easy AR demo with Xcode for you to have an idea of what you can build using ARKit. This demo shows a fighter jet in the air right in front of your device's camera.

- In order to see it working, first ensure your iOS device is chosen in the device picker dropdown menu at the top left hand corner of Xcode.

- Then, check the top menu bar in Xcode. Look for 'Product', tap it, and tap 'Run'.
- The top status indicator in Xcode should start flickering with messages and activity, then it should launch your app on your iOS device.
- To put a stop to your demo app, go back to 'Product' in Xcode and move down to 'Stop'.

With the above well followed, you are on your way to utilizing ARKit!

HOW TO SELECT TEXT

To select text on your iPad using your Apple Pencil:

- Access a Pages document, then click
- Click 'Apple Pencil', then switch on 'Select and Scroll'.

Perhaps your Apple Pencil backs it up, you can turn on double-click to switch, and then double-click the lower region of Apple Pencil to turn Select and scroll on and off.

To copy using your Apple Pencil:

- Select the object or text you want to copy
- Click 'Copy'. You may however have to click the selection again to see the copy.

- Right on the Home screen, open the app and file, note or message where you want to paste the selection
- Then, click Paste.

CAPTURE A NOTE FROM LOCKSCREEN

To achieve this, we would have to first add the Notes app to the control center. Once that is achieved, we can start a new note or probably access the former one based on the personalized settings. Worthy of note is the fact that this feature works seamlessly even on older versions like iOS 11 and 12.

To add notes to Control Center:

- Access the Settings app on your iOS or iPadOS device
- Click Control Center and select Customize Controls
- Right under the more controls section, find notes option and click on the +button to the left of it.
- Then, close the Settings app. You can now access Notes utilizing the control center of your device.

Access Notes on Lock Screen utilizing control center

Since you have added the Notes to the control center, you can simply get started with your notes right from the Lock screen.

- **On iPad and iPhone with Face ID:** swipe down from the top right corner to display the Control Center. Now, click on the Notes icon to get started
- **On iPhone and iPad with Touch ID-** swipe up from the bottom of the touch screen to display the Control Center and then click on the Notes icon to begin a new note or continue where you left off.
- Select whether to begin a New Note or Resume the Last one from lock screen

Automatically, iOS lets you begin a new note. However, you can decide to resume your last note. You can save the tips below for the times when you want to work on particular notes consistently.

- Access the Settings app on your device and click Notes.
- Then, move down and click 'Access Notes' from Lock Screen at the bottom.

Next, you are presented three options:

- Off: disable Notes access from the Lock screen

- Always Create New Note- select it to begin a new note from the Lock Screen
- Resume Last Note- choose it to continue with your last note.

Perhaps you chose "Resume Last Note", you will be presented the option to access the last note made on the Lock screen or viewed in the Notes app. You will need to go with the better option influenced by your needs.

Also, there exists an option to select the time duration after which you desire to create a new note. To provide a bit more security to your data, choose the shorter times because they are a bit more secure.

BEST APPS FOR APPLE PENCIL

Perhaps you have bought an Apple Pencil and desire to know the best apps to utilize with it, below are a few suggestions beyond the preloaded Notes app.

- **Cardflow**

You don't need a sticky note if you have Cardflow, as it performs the same function but digitally. You can make a wall of colored or plain pads, and scribble all the information and notes you need on them. It is a really speedy and simple way of organizing ideas, made easier by the Apple Pencil to organize and write with.

- **Scriptation**

This is an app that allows you to markup scripts, but it is not really an essential app for annotating all types of files, either they are documents to scrutinize or sign, or articles to criticize or analyze. There is a large range of tools to utilize and it is easy to import and export PDFs.

- **Autodesk SketchBook**

It is always essential to have an amazing art app. Perhaps you are feeling creative or just desire a great way of taking notes, Autodesk SketchBook remains one of the best. It possesses a wide collection of art tools, and also has a user interface that feels uniquely built for Apple Pencil with functions in all the right places.

HOW TO STORE YOUR PENCIL

The Apple Pencil is an amazing tool. A real designer's tool that feels good and right to hold. There is one challenge with the first generation Apple Pencil though, which has since been solved in the second-generation model, and that is the absolute fact that the Apple Pencil is absolutely cylindrical. This fact leads to a big issue- the Apple Pencil can roll away which can lead to it being damaged or lost.

So, how can you store your precious Pencil? Discussed below are some available accessories to make sure your stylus is well stored and secured.

- **Moxiware Magnet Sleeve**

This device has created a very Apple OE-esque set of sleeves for the Pencil, which offers it a secured attractable connection to your iPad Pro. It functions with an iPad 9.7" and iPad Pro 10.5 and 12.9".

- **Mildly magnetic iPad Smart Keyboard**

Perhaps you are using a smart Keyboard with your iPad Pro, you will notice that it is mildly attractable around the left-hand edge, and the Apple Pencil will just cling on to you. Although this is not a long-term storage strategy, it will prevent the Pencil from rolling away if you leave it on your desk.

- **Pencil clip hack**

Although this is an old one, it remains a good one. Reddit user texadoesitbest found out that the Pentel Sharp Automatic Pencil's detachable metal clip suits the Apple Pencil perfectly. Since it is chrome, it also matches the Pencil's shiny metal band.

- **Belkin Stand for Apple Pencil**

This offers you an elegant storage option to keep your stylus protected and stored even between uses. It holds the Apple Pencil upright and guides the tip while also permitting quick access to the device. The compact supplement is made of anodized aluminum and comes with a built-in bead-blasted finish that mirrors the minimal design of the Apple Pencil and iPad Pro, and appears great on your desktop.

- **Leuchtturm 1917 Pen Loop**

A premium notebook-maker Leuchtturm1917, which is the notebook taste of some of the CB offices, offers up for sale a handy pen loop to connect to its stationery. It is an item of quality, as befits the Leuchtturm1917 brand, which would make a perfect Apple Pencil holder.

The device appears neat and you can choose a color to fit your iPad Pro or Smart Cover's dominant hue- but all you need to do is pair it with the pencil clip hack, just to make sure that there is something hindering the Pencil from escaping, braces and belt, and all of that.

- **Stylus Sling**

The Stylus Sling remains a way to strap your Apple Pencil to your iPad to make sure that it is with you every time. A little utilitarian in design, it maxes on effectiveness and efficiency- and it possesses a little pocket into which you can slot the lightning connector, so you don't mislay that either.

LEARN HOW TO DRAW WITH IPAD AND APPLE PENCIL

The Apple Pencil is unique amongst the rest of the stylus crowd for some obvious reasons. They work hand in hand with Apple displays to produce low-latency brush strokes, they are both of more length than your normal digital pen, and they are charged through Lightning connector.

However, there are a few elementary techniques you need to know before you begin mastering your new tool, especially when it comes to drawing or writing. Discussed below is all you need to know when it comes to drawing with your Apple Pencil.

Drawspace - This boasts the catchword, "now everyone can draw", and perhaps it is perfect step-by-step drawing tutorials are anything to go by, that statement is the total truth.

Proko: Provides a bunch of amazing videos on drawing shapes and anatomy shapes.

Draw a box provides some interesting active tutorials for drawing day-to-day objects, landscapes, people, and of course- boxes.

The Postman's Knock is a website created to teach advanced calligraphy proficiency with a dip pen, and their printable PDFs are also amazing tools you can utilize to learn letter forms and figures.

Use your hand, your arm, hand and fingers can rest on the screen when you draw with Apple Pencil, thanks to the iPad's Palm-Rejection technology.

Learning in hand has an amazing resource for beginning to draw on the iPad, alongside some all-purpose guides to set up your workspace and drawing.

LEARN HOW TO DRAW FROM THE MASTERS

Perhaps you love the idea of an Apple Pencil but your drawing skills are not encouraging, practicing and drawing constantly might be the right advice for you. if you are just starting, looking at some of your preferred artists, getting acquainted with their styles, and making attempts to reproduce them on the digital canvas of your choice, might be the steps for you. it could be so much fun and should of course, get you thinking about styles and shapes.

Perhaps you want to learn right from the basics, there are a number of drawing apps and websites that provide great tutorials, PDFs, and videos.

Some of the apps are:

How to draw - This app does not endorse pressure for Apple Pencil, but the app provides nice guidelines for drawing popular animal shapes, and also doubles as a cool coloring app for upcoming artists.

ShadowDraw - This doesn't backup pressure sensitivity or tilt for Apple Pencil, but it contains a notable bunch of amazing tutorials to show you the methods of drawing in the style of different artists.

Calligraphy Penmanship - Though it is not the most properly designed app, and its pressure controls require some tweaking, it is a cool choice if you are looking to practice basic calligraphy forms.

How to Draw Everything- the library of this app contains a helpful step-by-step resource to learn how to draw anime, animals, game characters and other elements, although it has not been updated in a few years. You can't draw in the app, and it is not updated for Retina devices.

HOW TO MARKUP AN EMAIL WITH THE APPLE PENCIL

Apple has massively improved the way in which iOS and most apps work jointly with the Apple Pencil. For instance, in the mail app, you are able to include sketches and markup to emails you are presenting composing. That does not really help with incoming emails anyway, which likely stands for a majority of the emails that you want to markup. However, discussed below is a quick and convenient way to write directly on an email with the Apple Pencil:

What you need:

An iPad

GoodNotes 4

An Apple Pencil

An email that you want to mark up.

The very first thing to do is create a PDF from the email that you can, then markup using your Apple Pencil later. Although third-party email apps make it quite easy with a prominent share button and create PDF choices, Apple's own IOS Mail app conceals this behind some icons and a pinch-to-zoom gesture.

Step 1- press the Reply button

Access the email and click on the reply icon, which is situated at the upper right on the iPad.

Step 2- click Print

This is the first non-apparent option on iOS where you should be able to click a share icon instantly. 'Print' is the way to go in case of Mail.

Step 3- hit to create a PDF

This is exactly where the magic happens. After clicking the print button, a preview of the email will display. Pinch with your fingers as if you wanted to zoom out on the touchscreen right on that preview thumbnail. This will result in a PDF file from the chosen email.

Step 4- copy the PDF to GoodNotes

The generated PDF will eventually display the share button from where you can simply copy the created document to GoodNotes to mark up the email using your Apple Pencil or another stylus. GoodNotes will let you to either create a stand-alone document in any of your categories or append the email to an open notebook.

Step 5- Mark up the email using your Apple Pencil

Interestingly, you saved yourself an email that is awaiting mark up. You can utilize your Apple Pencil, your fingers or any other backed up stylus to write on the email as if you would have printed it out. Apparently, you can choose to either keep the annotated PDF in GoodNotes or export it to other apps of your choice.

HOW TO USE APPLE PENCIL WITH OFFICE 365 INK FEATURE ON YOUR IPAD PRO

The Apple Pencil works perfectly well with Office 365's new link feature so you can speed up markups on an iPad Pro.

Microsoft launched the newest edition of Office 365 sometime ago, and incorporated it as a new link feature that allows iPad Pro users use the Apple Pencil to markup presentations, documents, and spreadsheets easily. To utilize this feature, it demands $99 Apple Pencil ancillary and a perfectly compatible iPad Pro (presently in two sizes: the 12.9" and 9.7"). Discussed below are the ways to use this new feature on your iPad.

Utilizing the highlighter and pen features

To start utilizing the highlighted feature of the Microsoft Office apps, take these steps:

- Open Microsoft Word, Excel or PowerPoint.
- Access a document for editing
- Click the Draw tab
- Choose either the highlighter icon or the pen in the Draw tab

Start drawing anywhere on the document with the Apple Pencil paired with the iPad Pro. The pen tool or highlighter will make marks to imitate the real life tool.

Don't enable the option to 'Draw With Touch' when utilizing the Apple Pencil to prevent your hand or finger from pressing the screen and resulting in accidental marks.

Likewise, in the Draw tab, you can either choose the color utilizing the standard presets of red, green, black or blue, or for something more custom, choose the color wheel. You can also advance the line thickness of the drawn or sketched portion by clicking the + or − buttons to enable line thickness.

Adjusting the thickness or color will only alter new items drawn on the screen, and not formerly drawn items.

Erasing

This is as simple as drawing in the Office apps. Follow the listed steps to erase an already drawn line or highlight.

- Choose the Draw tab
- Choose the Eraser tool in the toolbar
- Draw over top of any highlight or formerly drawn pen mark.

This will completely erase highlights or any pen markings. Clicking a single line will erase the entire line by drawing over top of it.

Utilizing shape recognition

Shape recognition is integrated into Microsoft PowerPoint for iPad. It is easily used to create excellent shape renderings when utilizing the ink feature.

To utilize this feature, choose the 'Pen function', choose the color and thickness of the line, and track a circle, rectangle, oval, square, or triangle on the screen with the Apple Pencil. Make sure the choice to 'Convert to Shapes' is chosen. After sometime, the Office app will change over the roughly drawn shape into a flawless rendering of the shape you intend to draw.

WHEN YOU SHOULD REPLACE YOUR APPLE PENCIL NIB

For how long have you been using your Apple Pencil, for a year or more? Frequent use overtime results in the wear down of the tip and its gradual less responsiveness. It is not always apparent to tell when it is time for a replacement dissimilar to a normal lead pencil. You can verify the most appropriate time for a replacement considering the following factors.

- **When there is a large amount of friction**

Do you feel frequent friction when drawing on your iPad? The Apple Pencil should move across your screen without much drag even if you are utilizing a matte screen protector.

- **When you have been utilizing the same time for over a year**

Perhaps you use your Apple Pencil regularly and have owned it for over a year, there is a good chance that you are ready to replace the tip.

- **When brushes are not functioning as expected in Procreate.**

Do you observe little broken gaps in your brush strokes when utilizing Procreate? It could be a signal that it is time to change the tip of your Apple Pencil as long as you are not utilizing a brush that is created to do this of course.

- **When the tip is worn out and feels rough to touch.**

Move your finger around the tip of the Pencil to see how it feels. It is due for a replacement if the tip is rough to touch and the plastic is worn out.

- **When the pencil is less responsive**

The iPad responds so well to the Pencil. If you have to click quite hard, or re-click because the first click didn't register, you will be at the advantage side replacing the tip.

HOW DO I REPLACE MY APPLE PENCIL TIP?

Perhaps you are feeling a little nervous about changing your Pencil tip, be rest assured that it is a simple and straightforward process. To get this done, follow the steps below:

Step 1

In readiness for the task, get your replacement tip available nearby so you won't be moving around looking for it with a naked pencil with no tip.

Immediately you are ready, unscrew the used tip by turning it in a contra-clockwise motion.

Step 2

Withdraw your used Pencil tip from the base and put aside

Step 3

Position the replacement on the Pencil base and rotate it in a clockwise motion until it feels secure. You don't have to over-tighten it.

With the above steps, you have done a great job!

CONCLUSION

Perhaps you are new to the Apple Pencil or stylus gadgets generally; there are some things to know that could make your experience worthwhile.

Worthy of note is the fact that you don't need to press too hard with the stylus onto the screen to pick up inputs. However, the iPad comprehends how hard you press and many sketching apps and the likes will change the mark left influenced by the amount of pressure. A light touch is all that you need for a general note taking, and will further help protect the screen.

Perhaps you have the original Apple Pencil, charging it can be precarious- since it has to stick out from the iPad at a right angle, with just a little Lightning Connector sticking out. Therefore, it is advisable that you place your iPad down flat on a surface while the stylus charges, in order to prevent you from knocking the Apple Pencil and snapping the connector. Alternatively, remove the iPad out of the equation and utilize the supplied adapter for charging.

In addition, you should note that the Apple Pencil won't work for all functions on your device. Swiping up from bottom to bring up recent apps, or from the top to bring down the Control Center, for instance, will still function with your finger only. Taking note of this will prevent you from accidentally triggering the wrong function perhaps you draw to the edge of the screen with the stylus.

About the Author

Konrad Christopher is a video software expert with several years of experience in videography and software development. He is consistent following the latest development in the Tech and software industries and has an eye for high-end video equipment and software. He loves solving problems and he's enthusiastic about the software market.

Konrad holds a Bachelor's and MSc degree in software engineering from Cornell University, Ithaca. He lives in New York, USA. He is happily married with a kid.

Printed in Great Britain
by Amazon